This book
belongs to

The Miracle of Susie

The Puppy That Changed the Law

Susie's
HOPE

by Donna Lawrence

illustrations and cover design by Jennifer Tipton Cappoen

Book and Cover Designer: Jennifer Tipton Cappoen
Copy Editor: Lynn Bemer Coble
Photographers: Erin Arsenault, Jerry Wofford

Susie's
BOOKS

Susie's Books is an imprint of
Paws and Claws Publishing, LLC

1589 Skeet Club Road, Suite 102-175
High Point, NC 27265
www.PawsandClawsPublishing.com
info@pawsandclawspublishing.com

ISBN #978-0-9906067-2-7
Printed in the United States

Special Thanks...

I would like to thank my husband Roy and my family and friends for all of their support.

Thank you to everyone behind Susie's Law for all of their hard work and dedication.

A very special thank you to the wonderful people at the Guilford County Animal Shelter for saving Susie.

I also want to thank Roberta and Bob Wall for fostering Susie and for their help in nursing her back to health and in finding her a permanent home.

I would like to thank the man who found Susie in the park and cared enough to call for help.

I would also like to thank Ally Thomas with Southern Tails for all of the dog training that she has provided to Susie and me.

Most of all, I thank God for bringing Susie into my life at a time when I needed her the most.

~Donna Lawrence

This book is dedicated to all of the animals out there that had no voice but that now—thanks to Susie—have been given a voice.

Arise, shine; for thy light is come, and the glory of the Lord is risen upon thee.

Isaiah 60:1

Donna and Susie

Table of Contents

My name is Susie.

I was ten weeks old.
I was alone in a park.
I had no food and no water.
I ate trash and sticks.
It hurt when I chewed.

My owner had burned me and hurt my mouth.
My ears were just nubs.
I was really scared.
My burns itched.
I wanted to scratch.
When I did, they hurt.

For days, I walked in the park.
Flies buzzed around me.
Each morning the flies woke me up.
I was ready to give up.
I was getting close to dying.

At night I got really scared.

It was so dark.

I heard strange noises.

I hid under bushes.

I tried to make myself small.

I had bad dreams every night.

My owner was beating me.

He was burning me.

I woke up whimpering and sweating.

I was scared to go to sleep.

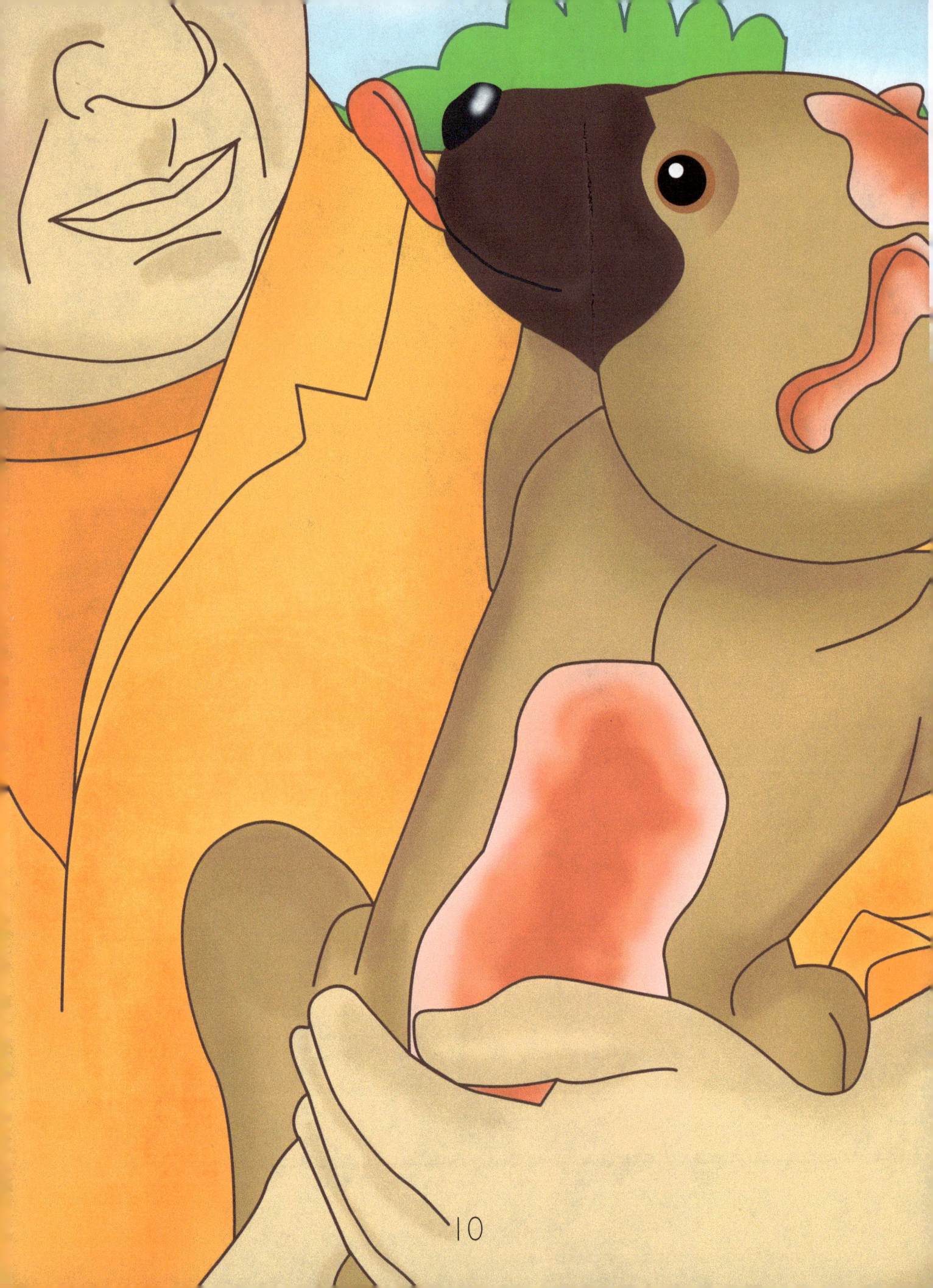

One day a man was walking in the park.

He saw me.

He stopped and got down on one knee.

He looked into my big, brown eyes.

He picked me up.

He held me close as he dialed his cell phone.

He said, "Don't give up, little girl.

Help is on the way.

You will be OK."

He hugged me.

I felt safe.

Soon a truck came.
Someone got out.

The caring man in the park gave me to them.
They carefully set me in a cage in the back.

We drove away.
I was so tired that I fell asleep.

We got to the animal shelter.

They carried me inside.

The veterinarian and vet tech stood around me.

They looked shocked.

They could not believe that someone had
done this to me.

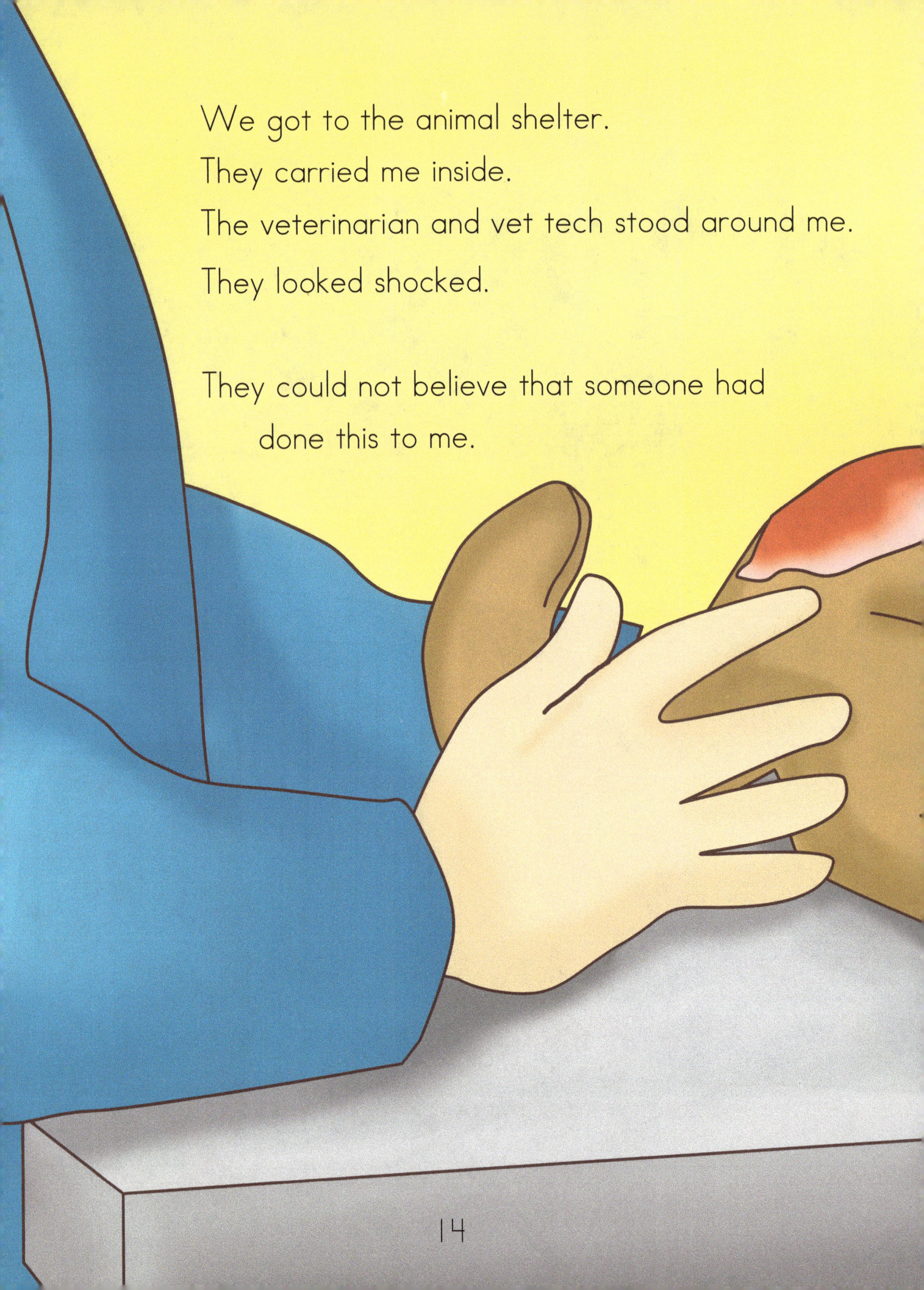

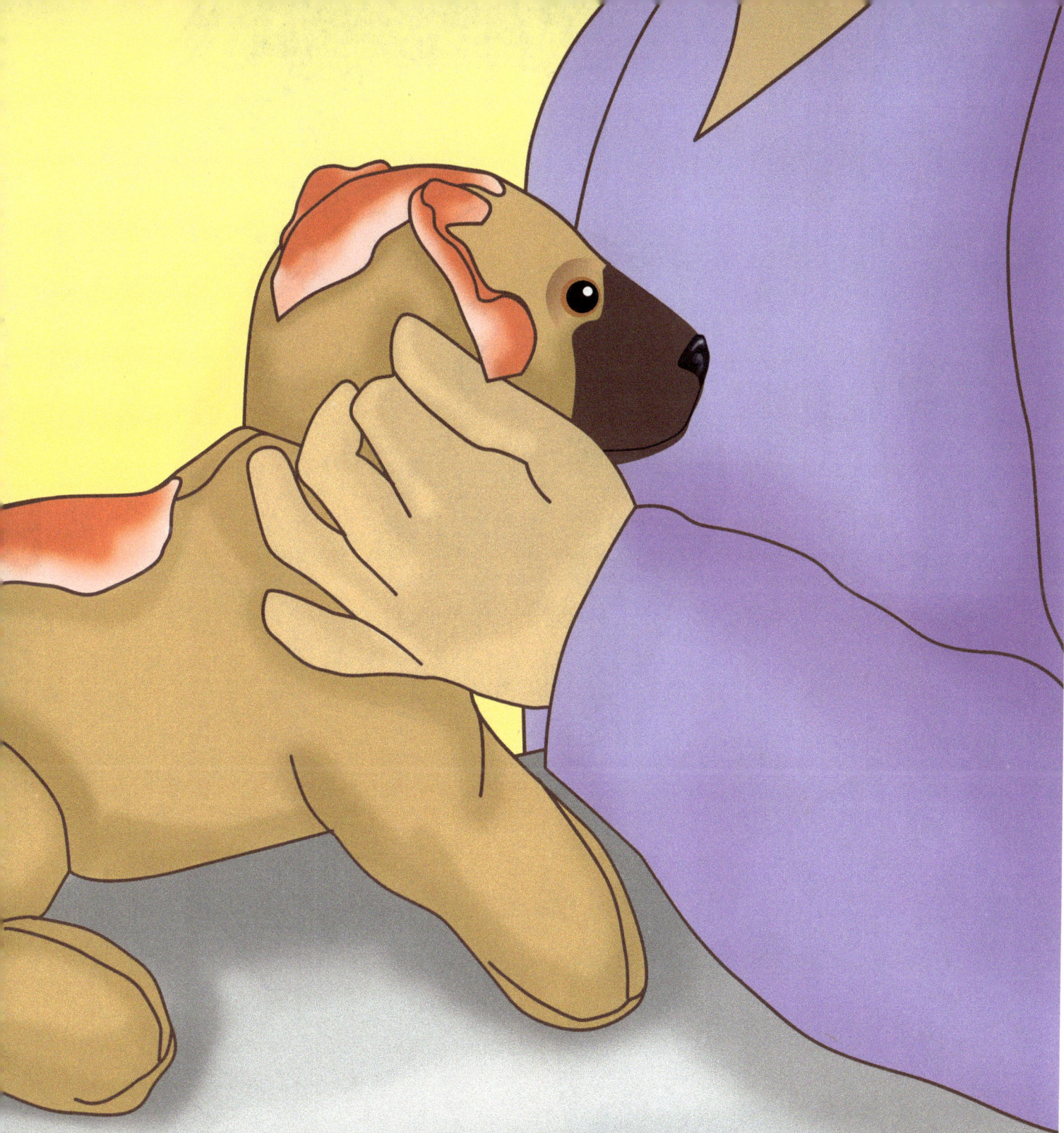

Everyone whispered, "Poor little puppy...Her jaw is broken...
She has missing teeth...And she has bad burns on most
of her body...Her ears are gone...Who could have
done this?...Who could have hurt her?...Poor baby."

They took me to a very bright room.
Everything was scary and shiny and silver.
I wanted the veterinarian to know that I would fight to live.
I looked into her eyes.
I licked her hand.
She said, "This little girl is a fighter.
We'll help her get better."

They found 300 maggots on my burns.
They took off each maggot.
They bathed me.
They cleaned my burns.
Then they bandaged them.
Everyone was gentle and careful.

I could only stay at the animal shelter
for a short time.
They had to find me a foster
home.
I needed medical care every
day for a long time.

Roberta and Bob Wall said they would
     foster me.
They took me home.
They had three white lapdogs and two cats.

My foster parents took care of my
     special needs.
They gave me a room of my own.
They loved me and cared for me.

My foster dad drove me to the
     Guilford County Animal
     Shelter.
There they did things my foster
     parents couldn't do.
At first we went every day.
     Then it was every other
     day.

At home my foster dad
     took maggots off
     my burns.
He was my hero. 18

My foster parents had a vacation coming.
They couldn't take me.
I still needed special care.

That was when Donna Lawrence got to know me.
She came every day during their vacation.
She watched movies with me in my room.
She rubbed my head.

My foster parents left directions for Donna.
The directions were for my special care and medicine.
Donna followed them exactly.
She drove me to the animal shelter for care.

Roberta and Bob came back home.

They had to find me a permanent home.

They had five other pets.

I needed my own family, place, and space.

They searched for my permanent home.

On the weekends, Donna helped them.

She took me to her home.

I got to lie around in her backyard.

Donna's dog was named Baby Girl.
I loved chasing Baby Girl.
We ran and ran.

24

I was a shepherd–pit bull mix.
Some people are afraid of pit bulls.
That made it hard to find me a home.

It was a long search.
Donna and her husband Roy decided to adopt me.
On moving day, my foster parents drove me to
    their home.
They took out my cage, toys, and clothes.
Then Baby Girl and I played more than ever.

I was home. I had my own home.
Donna and Roy had Baby Girl, seven cats, and me.

My first Christmas with them was special.
Donna gave gifts to Baby Girl and me.
She gave us costumes and toys.

One night Baby Girl and I were playing.
I growled.
Donna was terrified by that growl.
The next day she called Roberta and Bob.
She told them that she might have made
a mistake.

*I had to let Donna know that she didn't make
a mistake. I was meant to be in her home.*

About a year before Donna met me, her neighbors moved.

They didn't take their pit bull.

For years, they had chained the dog outdoors.

They had left it all alone.

They hadn't fed it enough food.

Donna felt sorry for the dog.

After they moved, she took food and water
     to the dog every morning.

One day the pit bull attacked her.

It locked her right leg in its teeth.

She kicked the dog off.

It jumped for her throat.

Donna held the dog in midair.

She threw the dog off her.

Then she ran to a neighbor's home.

He took her to the emergency room.

She got 45 stitches in her leg.

It took months for her to walk again.

That dog's attack was why my growl terrified
     Donna. Baby Girl and I were only playing.

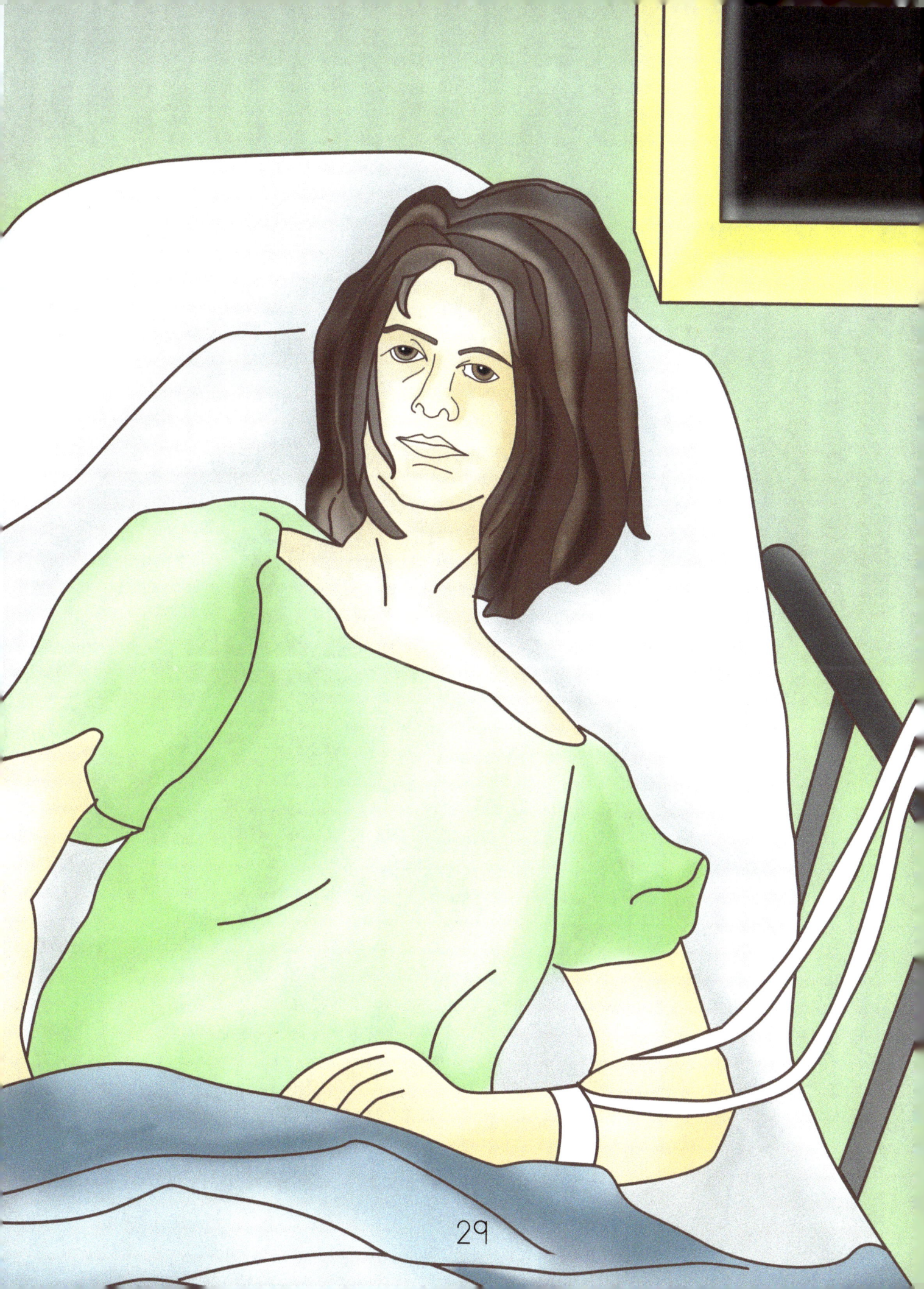

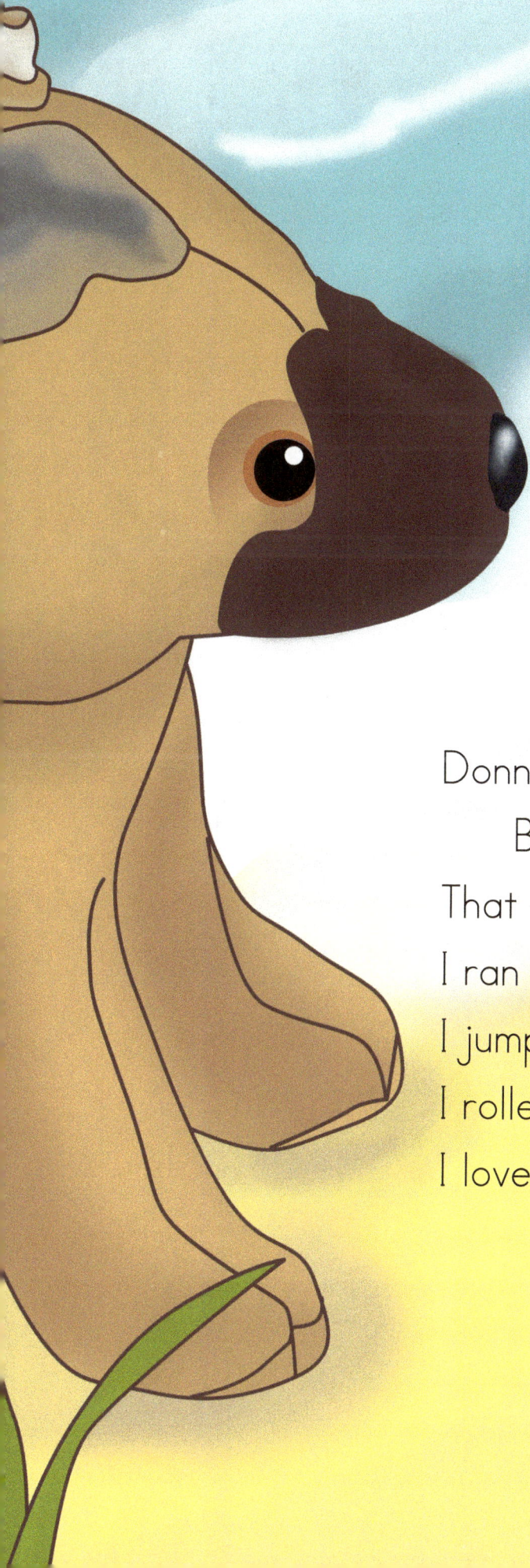

Donna and I went with Roberta and
    Bob on a summer beach trip.
That was my first beach trip.
I ran on the beach.
I jumped in the waves.
I rolled in the sand.
I loved the beach and the waves.

My mom and I have gone to schools.
We have gone to churches and to
    other groups.
My mom has told our stories.
We teach children how to take care of
    their pets.
We also teach them how to be safe
    around animals.
We have started the Susie's Hope™
    organization.
Through it, we spread our message.
It is the message of love, hope,
    and forgiveness.

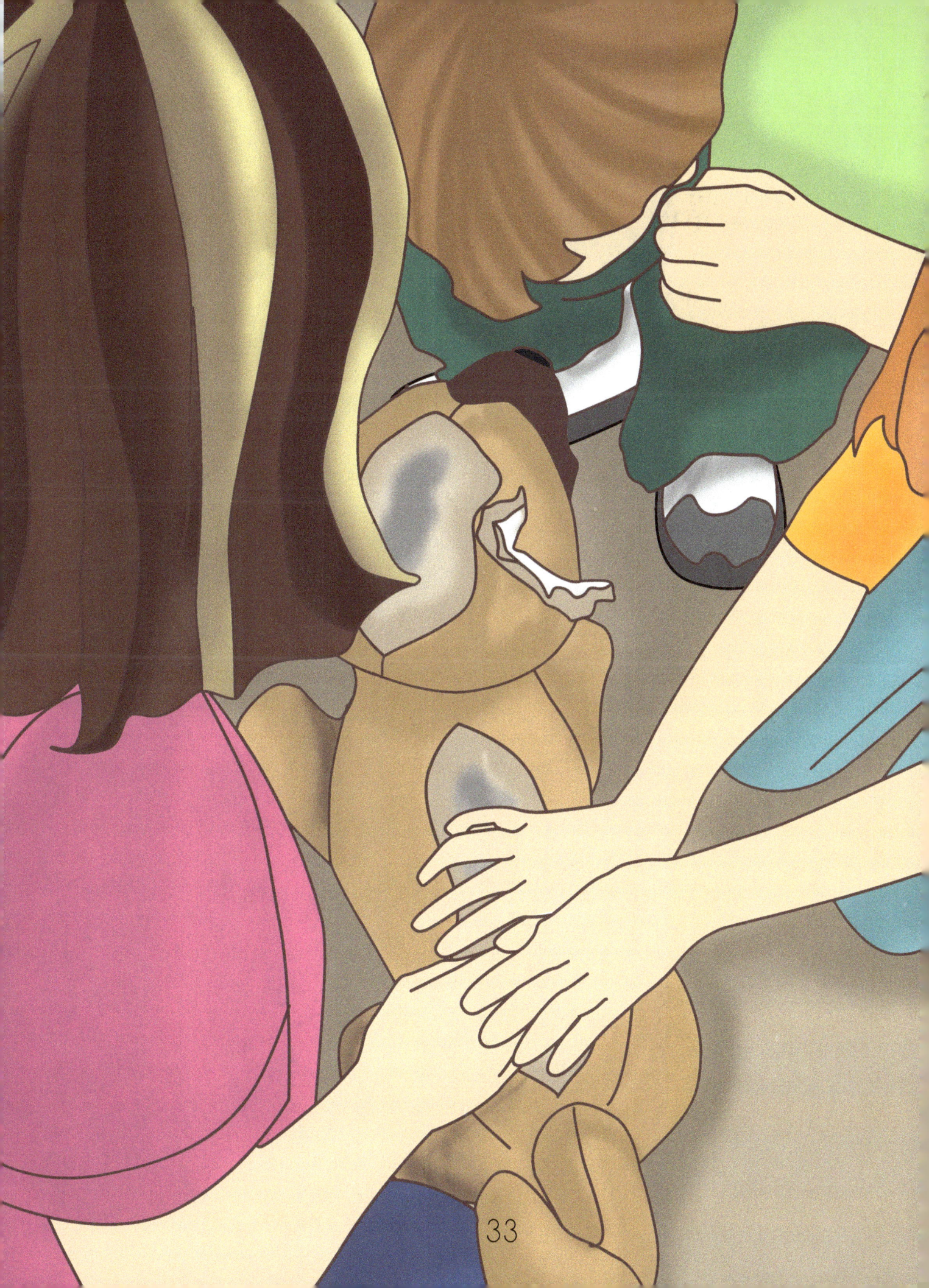

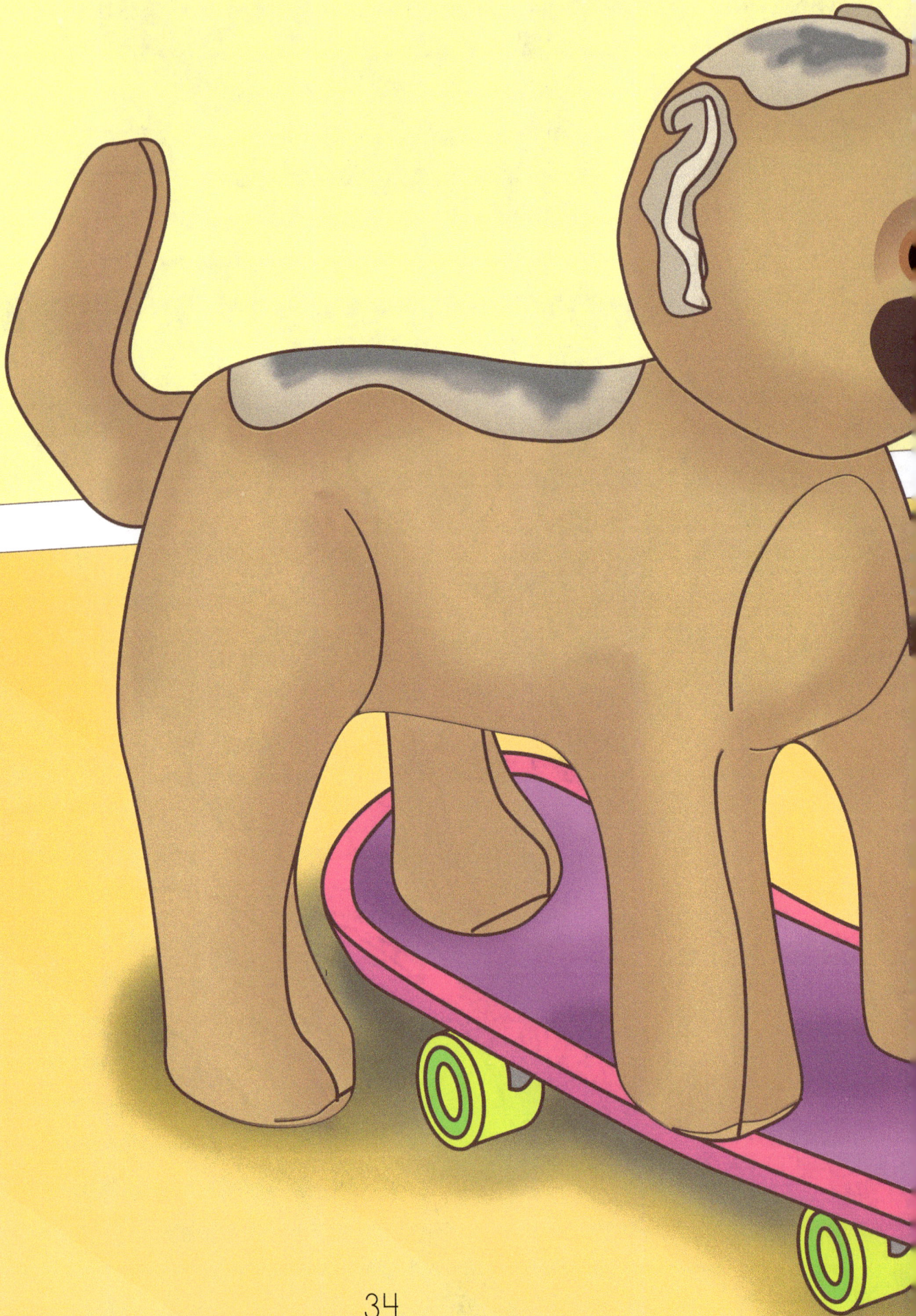

My trainer has taught my mom.
She has taught Mom how to teach
me to do tricks.
My mom and I have worked hard on
my training.

My mom taught me to ride a
skateboard.
She taught me to jump through hoops.

JDGE

My mom and I had our day in court.

I had to see the man who hurt me.

TV crews were there.

Lots of people came.

They were there for me.

My mom was proud that so many people came.

My mom, my foster mom, and others
wanted to make a new law.
They wanted the new law to let a judge give
jail time to people who hurt animals.

They got many people to write letters to our
state representatives.
People wrote E-mails too.
North Carolina Senator Don Vaughan
worked with us.
He helped us change the law.
He said to call it Susie's Law. I was excited
about that.
No one voted against it when the bill passed.

GENERAL ASSEMBLY OF NORTH CAROLINA
SESSION 2009

06-18-10

SENATE BILL 254
RATIFIED BILL

AN ACT TO INCREASE THE PENALTY FOR THE MALICIOUS ABU
KILLING OF AN ANIMAL.

The General Assembly of North Carolina enacts:

SECTION 1. G.S. 14-360(a1) reads as rewritten:
"(a1) If any person shall maliciously kill, or cause or procure to be
intentional deprivation of necessary sustenance, that person shall be
misdemeanor. Class H felony."

SECTION 2. G.S. 14-360(b) reads as rewritten:
"(b) If any person shall maliciously torture, mutilate, maim, c
poison, or kill, or cause or procure to be tortured, mutilated, maimed, cru
poisoned, or killed, any animal, every such offender shall for every such
Class I Class H felony. However, nothing in this section shall be cor
penalty for cockfighting provided for in G.S. 14-362."

SECTION 3. This act becomes effective December 1,
offenses committed on or after that date.
In the General Assembly read three times and ratified thi
2010.

Walter H. Dalton
President of the Senate

William L. Wainwright
Speaker Pro Tempore of t

Beverly E. Perdue
Governor

40

In June 2010, my mom and I went
    to Raleigh.
We went to the governor's mansion.
I had dressed up. My nails were painted pink.
My pearls were around my neck.
That was the first time I wore my pearls.

We met the governor.

The governor signed the bill in the back
    yard of the mansion.
My mom and I were beside her.
My paw print is on the bill. How cool is that!

Susie's Law went into effect in December
    2010.

Susie's

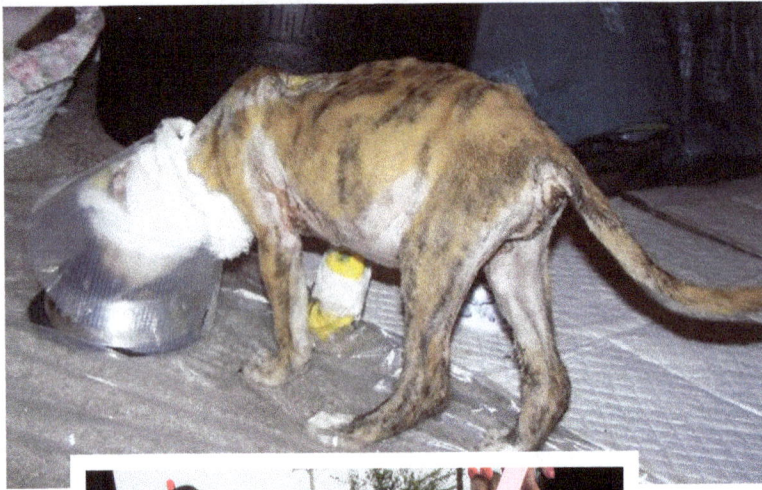

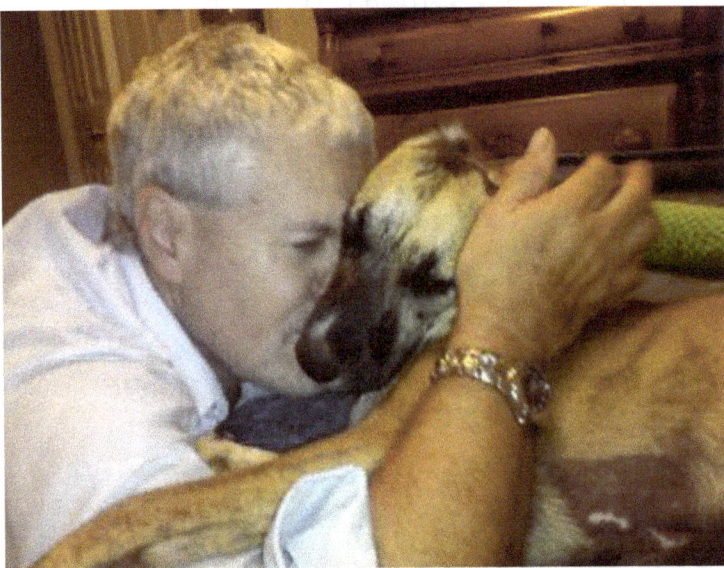

Photo Album

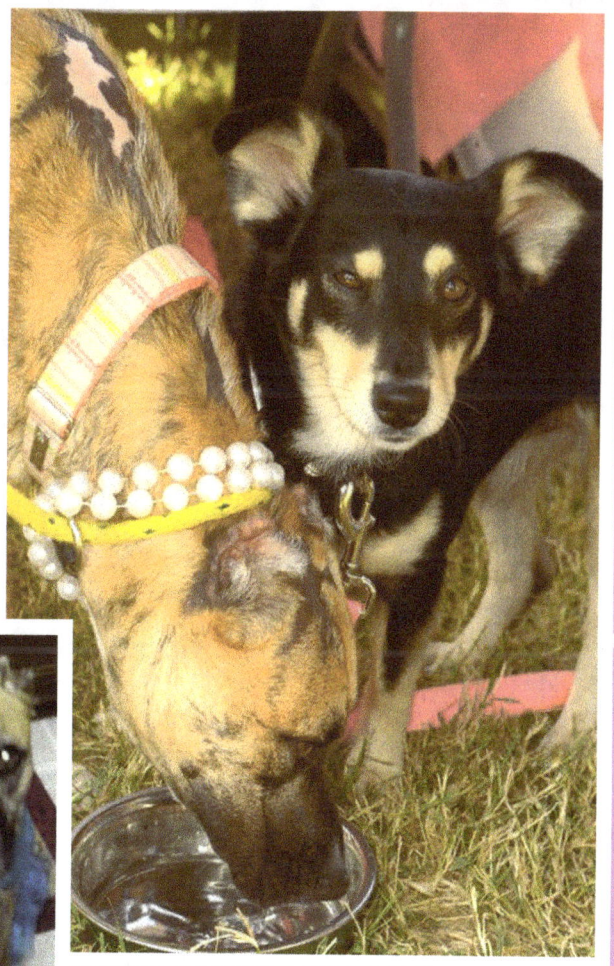

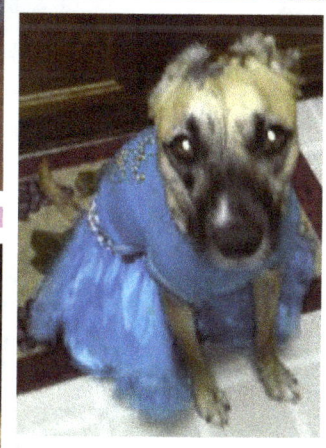

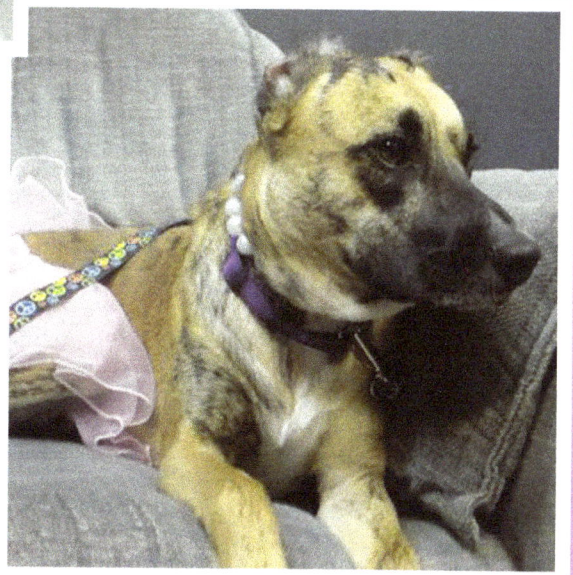

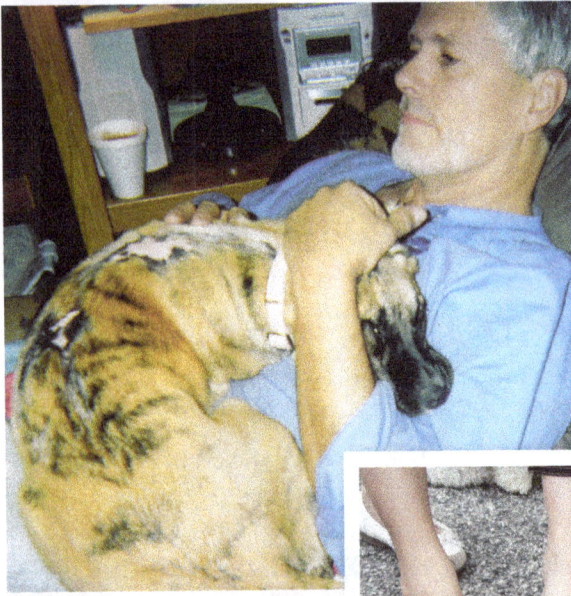

The Susie's Hope™ Program Is...

The Susie's Hope™ program features a powerful message of love, hope, and forgiveness.

It's about:
- Facing your fears and watching them disappear.
- Getting a second chance at life and running with it.
- Never giving up hope.
- Loving and trusting again.
- Moving forward and not looking back.
- Living for the moment and not living in the past.
- Not holding on to the negative in life, but focusing on the positive.
- Forgiving those who hurt you and in that way, going from being a victim to being a victor.

—⁂—

Susie and I are on a personal journey to educate and inspire people about the importance of animal safety and animal care. We have been working together as a team to motivate people to love and respect their pets. Education is the best prevention when it comes to animal abuse.

We have been visiting schools, churches, organizations, our special-needs community, pet adoption fairs, and fund-raisers. Soon we hope to visit hospitals and medical facilities to inspire burn victims and cancer patients, along with victims of any kind of violence and abuse.

—⁂—

We tell the story of two miracles—human and animal. Susie and I both survived a brutal attack and lived to tell about it.

~Donna

Susie's Hope™ Pledge

I, _____, on this

_____ day of _____

promise never to abuse, neglect, torture, or bring harm in any way to any kind of animal. I will love and respect all of God's creatures big and small.

To care for my pet, I will provide shelter, water, food, exercise, groomings, and regular checkups. I promise to love and respect my animal and to take care of my pet to the best of my ability.

Hand with paw, I will honor Susie's Law.

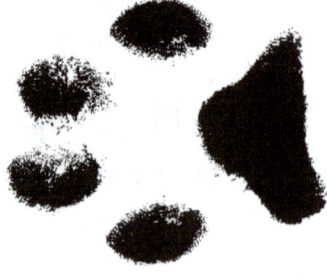

_____
Susie's Signature

_____
Signature

Donna Lawrence
Donna's Signature

I am Susie. I am a survivor.
I am the voice for all abused and
neglected animals.
Together Donna and I are
spreading the message of love,
hope, and forgiveness.

Instrumental People

Dr. Ashley Spruill

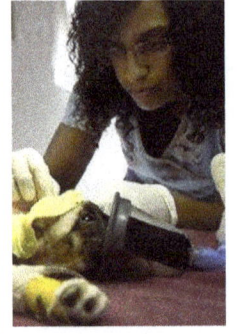

Vet Tech
Marissa Lea Stadivent

Guilford County Animal Shelter staff—Second from
left: Director Marsha Williams

Foster parents Roberta
and Bob Wall

Susie's trainer
Ally Thomas

Christopher L. Parrish
Assistant District Attorney for the
State of North Carolina in the
18th Prosecutorial District

Susie's Team

Left to Right: House Representative Pricey Harrison, House Representative Maggie Jeffus, Senator Don Vaughan, *(behind)* House Representative Laura Wiley, House Representative Alma Adams, Governor Bev Perdue, Donna Lawrence, and Susie

Susie's Hope™ Team

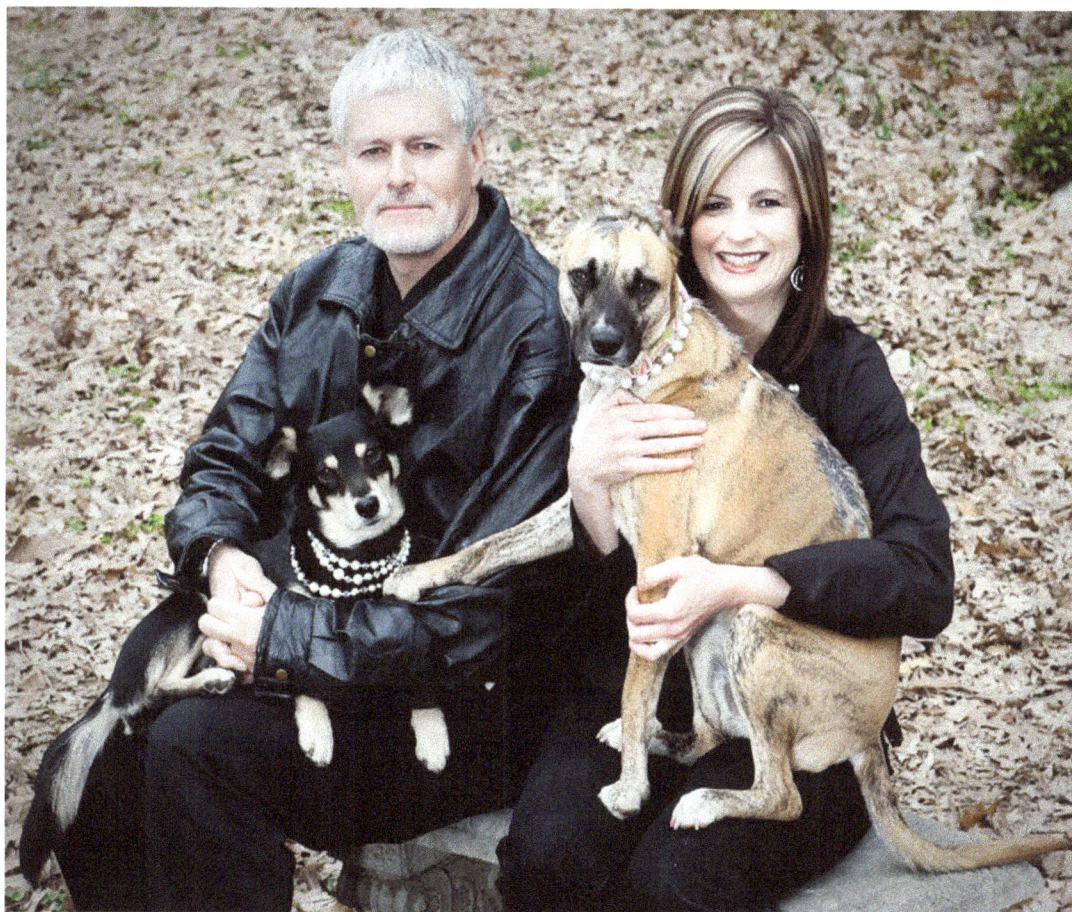

The Lawrences: Roy, Baby Girl, Donna, and Susie

In Susie's Words

One day a human hurt me really bad.
But to tell you what happened would make you sad.

Instead I will tell you a happy tale
Of all the loving people who made me well.

My friends at the shelter doctored me up
And made me once again a healthy pup.

As I got better, family and friends pitched in
To make sure I was healthy and happy again.

My forever mom, Donna, gave me a home
With unconditional love I had never known.

To keep my animal friends safe, no matter how small,
Hand with paw, Susie's Team and friends changed the law.

A happy ending is what we should share
With all of God's creatures, big and small, everywhere.

So love and respect your pets, and treat them right.
It's time to cuddle up with my mom and say goodnight.

~Susie

About the Author and Susie

Donna Lawrence is a native of Pine Hall, North Carolina. She was raised on a farm with her parents and seven brothers and sisters. For 20 years, Donna has been the owner and manager of The Kutting Edge salon in Greensboro.

In October 2008, Donna was attacked by a pit bull and nearly died. Understandably, the attack left her extremely fearful of dogs, but that changed in August 2009. That is when she met Susie, the puppy that had been found beaten, burned, and left to die in a Greensboro, North Carolina, park. Susie has helped Donna overcome her fear of dogs and has given Donna new inspirations for life.

Donna is the Founder and Executive Director of the Susie's Hope™ nonprofit organization that educates children and adults about the importance of animal care and safety.

—⁂—

Susie resides with her mom and dad in High Point, North Carolina. Susie's tragic story became the motivation and inspiration behind Susie's Law that went into effect in North Carolina on December 1, 2010. Susie is a brindle pit bull–shepherd mix. She was adopted by Roy and Donna Lawrence from the Guilford County Animal Shelter on December 8, 2009. The Lawrences have helped Susie learn to love and respect humans who love and respect her.

About the Artist

Jennifer Tipton Cappoen has a bachelor's degree in fine arts from the University of North Carolina at Greensboro. She has spent more than 25 years honing her skills as an illustrator and a designer for both the educational and Christian publishing markets. Her work has been featured in publications by The Education Center, Inc.; New Day Publishing; True Hope Publishing Inc.; Laurus Books; and Bayard Publishing. She lives in Greensboro, North Carolina, with her husband, Andrew, and their four dogs. Their dog Crickett died before we created this book.

Susie and I both say to her abuser,
"You are forgiven."

www.ingramcontent.com/pod-product-compliance
Lightning Source LLC
Chambersburg PA
CBHW081302040426
42452CB00014B/2621